Nurses Joke Book

The Ultimate Collection of Nurses Jokes

By Chester Croker

Jokes For Nurses

These jokes for nurses will make you giggle. Some of these jokes are old, some of them are new and we hope you enjoy our collection of the very best nurse jokes and puns around.

This huge collection of the very best nurse jokes and puns will prove that nurses have a great sense of humor, and these jokes are guaranteed to make you giggle.

There are some great one-liners to start with, plenty of quick fire question and answer themed gags, many story led jokes, a number of risqué jokes, some funny junior nurse mistakes and plenty of nurse patient exchanges all designed to get you laughing.

Published by Glowworm Press
7 Nuffield Way
Abingdon OX14 1RL

FOREWORD

When I was asked to write a foreword to this book I was flattered.

That is until I was told by the author, Chester Croker, that I was the last resort, and that everyone else he had approached had said they couldn't do it!

I have known Chester for a number of years and his ability to create funny jokes is remarkable. He is incredibly quick witted and an expert at crafting clever puns and amusing gags and I feel he is the ideal man to put together a joke book about our wonderful profession.

He once told me, "When you're a nurse you know that every day you will touch a life, or a life will touch yours."

He will be glad you have bought this book, as he has an expensive lifestyle to maintain.

Enjoy!

Ian Payne

Table of Contents

Chapter 1: One Liner Nurse Jokes

The nurse who can smile when things go wrong.....is probably going off duty.

You should always be kind to nurses. Remember they choose your catheter size.

Elves and nurses do have something in common. We do all the work and one guy in an over-sized coat gets all the credit.

I remember the fear of realizing on the first day of nursing school that watching every episode of ER would get me nowhere.

When I went to get my vaccinations the young nurse told me she was very nervous as it was her first time. I told her to give it her best shot.

Transplant nurses hate rejection.

You know you are a nurse when you find yourself betting on a patient's blood alcohol content.

When I am at the mall, I avoid unhealthy looking people for fear that I may have to administer CPR on my day off.

Attractive nurses probably never get accurate pulse readings from their patients. Mind you, neither do ugly ones.

A nurse wakes up her patient and says, "Wake up Madam, it's time to take your sleeping pills."

Treat your nurse well. She can walk as slowly or as fast as she chooses to retrieve that pain medication you requested.

Did you hear about the cross eyed nurse who got sacked because she couldn't see eye to eye with her patients.

Midwife for sale.

Can Deliver.

Nursing would be a dream job if there were no doctors or patients.

I love nursing school, care plans and final exams. Said no-one ever.

Nurses are the beating heart of our medical system.

How come waitresses serve food and get tipped 18%, but I regularly, scrub feet, provide medicine and keep people alive and get no tips at all?

Did you hear about the student nurse who stole a calendar? She got twelve months.

Multiple traumas – A unit full of ventilators and patients trying to die on me all day...I'm sorry what were you saying about your busy day with the stapler?"

A practical nurse is one who marries a rich, terminally ill patient.

When you are in hospital, your friends ask, "How are you?" But your best friend asks, "How is the nurse?"

A psychotic mechanic in a mental hospital had sex with a nurse then he escaped. The headline in the paper the next day was 'Nut screws and bolts.'

Laughter is not the best medicine - Propofol is.

The nurse told me not to worry about bird flu. She said it's tweetable.

Last week, my husband wanted to spice things up a little, and he suggested that we play doctors and nurses. So I strapped him to a trolley, put him in the hallway, and ignored him for 48 hours.

Did you hear about the nurse who died and went straight to hell? It took her two weeks to realize that she wasn't at work anymore.

Statistically 9 out of 10 injections are in vein.

A ward sister instructs a group of junior nurses, "Be patient with patients who are not patient."

Nursing: Expose yourself to rare, exotic and exciting new diseases daily.

Nursing school is a lot like giving birth; once it's over, you just tend to forget just how painful the process really was.

As a trauma nurse, patients stupidity is my job security.

I was called pretty today. Actually, the full sentence was, 'You're a pretty bad nurse' but I'm choosing to focus on the positive.

Nursing: Where else can you experience the thrill of having total strangers poop in front of you like it's totally your business?

Most nurses refer to motorcyclists as 'organ donors.'

Welcome to Nursing School: Where every week feels like finals week.

The nurse taking my blood got annoyed when I told her that she was bad at her job. I don't understand why though, as all she kept saying was, "Be negative."

The nurse told her patient to stop using a Q-tip, but it went in one ear and out the other.

How can anybody hate nurses? Nobody hates nurses. The only time you hate a nurse is when they're giving you an enema.

'Code Brown' does not mean that the patient has brought you a box of chocolates.

Always thank your nurse. Sometimes they're the only one between you and a hearse.

Nursing is not a career - it's a post-apocalyptic survival skill.

Chapter 2: Question and Answer Nurse Jokes:

Q: Why was the nurse shouting Typhoid, Measles, Tetanus?

A: *She likes to call the shots.*

Q: Why do nurses bring red pens into work?

A: *In case they have to draw blood.*

Q: What do you call two ITU nurses holding hands?

A: *A synapse.*

Q: What is the opposite of you're out?

A: *Urine.*

Q: What did the nurse say when she found a rectal thermometer in her pocket?

A: *"Some asshole has my pen."*

Q: What is it called when a hospital runs out of maternity nurses?

A: *A mid-wife crisis.*

Q: Why do nursing homes give Viagra to the old men every night?

A: *It keeps them from rolling out of bed.*

Q: Why did the doctor tell the nurse to walk quietly past the medicine cabinet?

A: *So she wouldn't wake the sleeping pills.*

Q: What's the difference between a nurse and a nun?

A: *A nun only serves one God.*

Q: Why did the nurse keep the bedpan in the refrigerator?

A: *Because when she kept it in the freezer it took too much skin off.*

Q: When is the worst time to have a heart attack?

A: *During a game of charades.*

Q: What Does LPN Stand For?

A: *Low paid nurse.*

Q: What do nurses watch at the old folks home?

A: *The Grammies.*

Q: How do you tell the difference between a nurse and a lawyer?

A: *By how they pronounce the word invalid.*

Q: What do you call the Imodium the head nurse at Hogwarts gives you?

A: *Defense against the Dark Farts.*

Q: What did the nurse tell her patient after he refused to let her mend a cut on his arm?

A: *"Fine; suture self."*

Q: What's the difference between an oral thermometer and a rectal thermometer?

A: *The taste.*

Q: What do you get if you have strep throat on Friday?

A: *Saturday Night Fever.*

Q: How long does it take a nurse to change a light bulb?

A: *About 15 seconds to change it and 20 minutes to document it – how, when, where, why, and what serial number it had.*

Q: How many triage nurses does it take to change a light bulb?

A: *One, but the bulb will have to spend four hours in the waiting room.*

Q: How many doctors does it take to change a light bulb?

A: *Only one, but he has to have a nurse to tell him which end to screw in.*

Q: How many physiotherapists does it take to change a light bulb?

A: *None. They just give the dead bulb exercises to do and hope it will be working better the next time they see it.*

Q: What is 40 feet long and smells like urine?

A: *Line dancing at a nursing home.*

Q: How do you know that a dead body found by the side of the road is a nurse?

A: *Because its stomach is empty, its bladder is full, and its ass has been chewed.*

Q: What do you call a friendly Mancunian midwife?

A: *Ultra sound.*

Q: What did the old man say to the prettiest nurse at the nursing home?

A: *"I've fallen for you and I can't get it up."*

Q: How do you save a doctor from drowning?

A: *Take the nurse's foot off his head.*

Q: Why did the cannibal nurse get disciplined?

A: *For buttering up the patients.*

Q: What did the nurse say to the patient who swallowed some Scrabble tiles?

A: *"Don't worry; you'll have a vowel movement soon."*

Q: What's the difference between a surgeon and a puppy?

A: *If you put a puppy in a room by itself for an hour, it'll probably stop whining.*

Q: Why is Hercules the most suitable midwife out of all the demigods?

A: *Because he's already been through 12 labours.*

Q: What do transplant nurses hate?

A: *Rejection.*

Q: Why do nurses go to art school?

A: *To learn how to draw blood.*

Chapter 3: Shorter Nurse Jokes

A hospital nurse caring for a man from Kentucky asked him, "How's your breakfast this morning?"

He replied, "It's very good, except for the Kentucky Jelly. I just cannot get used to the taste."

The nurse was puzzled and asked to see the jelly.

The patient then produced a foil packet labeled 'KY Jelly.'

A hospital posted a notice in the nurses' lounge that said, 'Remember, the first five minutes of a human being's life are the most dangerous.'

Underneath, a nurse had written, 'The last five are pretty risky, too.'

A man rushed into a hospital and asked a nurse for a cure for hiccups.

Grabbing a cup of water, the nurse quickly splashed it into the man's face.

"What did you that for?" screamed the man.

The nurse said, "You don't have the hiccups now, do you?"

"No I don't," replied the man. "My wife out in the car has them."

A nurse notices one of her hospital patients is in a panic so she asks what's wrong.

He says, "I'm due to have an operation but I over-heard the nurse say, 'It's a very simple operation, don't worry, I'm sure it will be all right.'"

The nurse says, "What's so scary about that?"

The guy replies, "She was talking to the surgeon."

A brigadier decides to visit the psychiatric ward of an army hospital.

He wants to find out how they decide if a soldier needs to be admitted as a patient or to be just seen as an out-patient.

The QA psychiatric nurse explains, "We fill a bath with water and give the soldier a mess tin and a spoon. They are then asked to empty the bath s quickly as they can."

"I see," exclaims the brigadier. "A normal person would use the mess tin because it is much larger than a spoon and it would thus take less time to empty the bath."

"No Sir," sighs the psychiatric nurse. "A sane person would simply pull the bath plug out. I'll get your bed ready, Sir."

Upon leaving the hospital after the birth of my son, a nurse in the elevator commented on him sucking on my finger saying, "He's quite the little sucker."

I responded, "There's one born every minute."

A worried charge nurse said, "Doctor, the man you just gave a clean bill of health to dropped dead just as he was leaving the hospital."

The doctor replied, "Turn him around. Make it look like he was walking in."

While visiting a friend in the hospital, I noticed several gorgeous nurses were all wearing a pin designed to look like an apple.

I asked one of them, "What does the pin signify?"

"Oh, nothing," she replied with a chuckle. "We just use them to keep the doctors away."

I was visiting my partner in hospital when the nurse suggested that it might help if I adjusted her pillows to make it more comfortable.

The nurse was right.

After I took the pillows and put them on my chair, I was a lot more comfortable.

Two senior nurses are talking about sex.

One says to the other that she reckons sex is 75% work and 25% pleasure.

The other nurse reckons that sex is 25% work and 75% pleasure.

They decide to ask the student nurse for her opinion.

"Sex is all pleasure" says the student nurse.

"Why do you say that?" ask the other two.

The student nurse replies, "Because if it there is any work involved, you two have me do it."

My brother, who uses a wheelchair, turned up recently at the hospital for an appointment.

The charge nurse checked the schedule, and then said, "The nurse will call you in a moment. Please have a seat."

He smiled and immediately said, "Done."

A doctor asked a novice blonde nurse, "Did you take the patient's temperature?"

The blonde nurse replies, "No, is it missing?"

One of the nurses came over when to me she saw I was crying in the waiting room.

"What's wrong?" she asked.

"I don't believe it," I wept, "I reversed my car into my mother-in-law."

The nurse replied, "Sir, I can assure you that she'll be perfectly fine."

I said, "Exactly."

A nurse comes into the doctor's waiting room and says to the group of people waiting, "Due to new GDPR privacy rules I am not allowed to call you by your names. So, can the patient with syphilis, please come in."

It was time for my annual checkup.

Following the nurse's instructions, I collected a stool sample and put it in a plastic container before we left for the health center.

When I arrived, I handed the sample to the receptionist, who immediately cracked a smile.

The container read. 'I Can't Believe It's Not Butter.'

A young nurse is relaxing at a bar after work one night, when a large sweaty construction worker comes in and sits down next to her.

They begin to chat and eventually the conversation gets on to nuclear war.

The nurse asks the construction worker, "If you hear the sirens go off, and you know the missiles are on their way, and you've only got twenty minutes or so left to live, what would you do?"

He replies, "I am going to make the most of those twenty minutes, and make it with anything that moves."

The construction worker then asks the nurse what she would do to which she replies, "I'm going to keep perfectly still."

After my proctology exam I was left alone in the exam room for a few minutes.

A nurse then came in and said three words no man ever wants to hear.

She said, "Who was that?"

A dog walks into a pub, takes a seat and says to the barman, "Can I have a glass of Prosecco please."

The barman has never heard a talking dog and is stunned.

He says, "Wow, that's incredible - you should join the circus."

The dog replies, "Why? Do they need nurses?"

A very upset man spoke to his nurse friend.

"You've got to help me." he howled.

She said, "What seems to be the trouble?"

He replied, "I keep having the same dream, every night. There's this door with a sign on it, and I push and push the door but I can't get it open."

She asks, "What does the sign say?"

He replies, "Pull."

A nurse had to take an elderly patient back to her room after surgery.

The woman was still feeling the effects of the anesthetic and was rather confused.

After the nurse had made her comfortable, the nurse met one of the patient's friends who asked, "How is she?"

The nurse replied, "Oh, she's quite dopey."

The friend said, "I know that, but how is she health wise?"

A senior nurse tells her patient, "Which do you want first, the good news or the bad news?"

The patient replies, "Give me the good news."

The nurse says, "You're about to have a disease named after you."

A nurse took her cross-eyed Rottweiler to the vet.

The vet picked the dog up to examine him and said, "Sorry, I'm going to have to put him down."

The nurse said, "Oh no. Is it that bad?"

The vet replied, "No, he's just very heavy."

The maternity nurse told the parents of a newly born child, "You have a beautiful baby."

The beaming husband said, "I bet you say that to all new parents."

"No," she replied, "only to those whose babies really are good-looking."

The husband asked, "So what do you say to the other parents?"

The nurse replied, "The baby looks just like you."

I got a phone call last night to say that my wife had been in an accident.

I rushed to the hospital and asked the nurse, "How is she, can I see her?"

She looked at me sadly and said, "I'm afraid you're too late."

I said, "Okay, no problem. I'll come back in the morning."

A nurse is late for duty and is unable to find a parking space at the staff car park.

"Lord," she prayed. "If you open up a space up for me, I swear I'll give up drinking and go to church every Sunday."

Suddenly, the clouds part a ray of sunshine beams down onto an empty parking spot.

Without any hesitation, the nurse said out loud, "Never mind Lord, I've found one."

I took my son to the hospital after he swallowed some coins.

He was rushed into surgery.

An hour or so later I saw a nurse so I asked her how my son was.

She said, "There's no change yet."

A family brings their elderly mother to a nursing home.

A nurse bathes her and puts her in a chair by the window.

After a while, she slowly starts to lean over sideways in her chair.

An attentive nurse immediately straightens her up.

Again, she starts to tilt to the other side.

The nurse rushes back to put her upright.

This goes on several times during the morning.

At 1pm, the family arrives and one of them asks, "Are they treating you well?"

"Yes," the old woman replies. "Except they won't let me fart."

A nurse enters the room of a difficult patient who demands to know the results of his examination.

She tells him, "I'm afraid I have some bad news. You're dying and you don't have much time."

The man says, "Oh no, that's dreadful news. How long have I got?"

"10..." says the nurse.

"10? 10 what? Months? Weeks? What?" he asks desperately.

She replies, "10...9...8...7..."

A young woman wearing Gothic clothing, numerous tattoos and with an orange Mohican punk rocker hairstyle bursts into the hospital complaining of abdominal pain.

The nurse established that the patient had acute appendicitis, so she was booked in for immediate surgery.

When she was completely disrobed on the operating table, the staff observed that her pubic hair had been dyed green, and above it, there was a tattoo that read, "Keep off the grass."

After the surgery had been completed, the surgeon wrote a short note on the patient's dressing, which said, "Sorry, but I had to mow the lawn."

A woman went for a routine physical examination at the hospital.

The nurse handed her a urine specimen container and said, "The bathroom is on your left. The doctor will be with you in a few minutes."

A few minutes later the lady came out of the bathroom with a relieved look on her face and an empty container.

She said to the nurse, "Thank you, but there was a toilet in there, so I didn't need this container after all."

A retired guy who volunteers to entertain patients in nursing homes went to one place and took his guitar along with him.

He told some stories and sang some songs.

As he was leaving, he said, "I hope you get better."

One elderly gentleman replied, "I hope you get better, too."

I went to casualty yesterday and told the nurse, "I've been stung by a bee, have you got anything for it?"

She asked, "Whereabouts is it?"

I said, "I don't know, it could be miles away by now."

A policeman was rushed to the hospital with an inflamed appendix.

The doctors operated and afterwards advised him that all was well.

However, the cop kept feeling something pulling at the hairs on his chest.

He decided to pull his hospital gown down enough so he could see what was making him so uncomfortable.

Taped firmly across his hairy chest were four wide strips of adhesive tape, the kind that doesn't come off easily.

Written in large black letters was the sentence, 'Get well soon. From the nurse you gave a ticket to last week.'

A man speaks hysterically into the phone, "My wife is pregnant, and her contractions are only a couple of minutes apart."

"Is this her first child?" the nurse queries.

"No, you fool," the man screams. "This is her husband!"

At the hospital, on the battlefield a severely wounded General was carried in.

The doctor immediately started operating on the General in an attempt to save his life.

During the surgery, the nurse was acting strangely.

All of a sudden, the nurse took out a knife and stabbed the doctor in the heart.

While crying, the nurse said, "I'm very sorry doctor. You've always treated me well and I am very fond of you, but I'm actually a spy and I cannot let you save the life of this man."

While clutching his wound, the doctor replied, "You idiot. Why didn't you just stab the General instead?"

A man is in hospital bed wearing an oxygen mask over his mouth.

The nurse hears him mumble, "Are my testicles black?"

She lifts his gown, holds his manhood in one hand and his testicles gently in the other while she takes a closer look.

She then says, "There's nothing wrong with them, Sir."

The guy pulls off his oxygen mask, smiles at her and says, "Thanks for that, that was lovely but what I actually said was 'Are my test re-sults back?'"

After my prostate exam, the man in the white coat left me alone.

A few minutes late, the nurse came in, with a worried look on her face, and said the three words I was dreading to hear.

She said, "Who was that?"

A man wakes up in hospital from surgery, and asks the nurse, "Were you able to save my testicles?"

She replied, "Yes, we saved them for you. They are in a jar next to you on the bed-side table."

An Asian nurse goes in to see a patient who has rung his bell.

A few minutes later she storms out, stating she refuses to deal with such a racist patient.

The doctor asks the patient what he said to upset the nurse.

He says, "I have no idea. She asked me if anything was bothering me, and I just said yeah, urination."

The nurse brought me my new-born baby and said, "I'm sorry, your wife didn't make it."

I immediately handed it back to the nurse and told her to bring me the one my wife had made.

A priest has a heart attack, and is rushed into hospital.

He wakes up as he's being pushed through the hospital on a trolley by two nurses.

The disoriented priest asks, "Am I in heaven?"

"No," says one of the nurses. "We're just taking a short cut through the children's ward."

After my wife had given birth to our first baby, the nurse asked me, "Do you have a name yet?"

I grinned and said, "Yes, Alexander."

She gushed, "That's a lovely name."

"Thanks," I said. "But what do you think we should call the baby?"

A young boy was brought into the emergency room after swallowing part of a plug-in air freshener.

After consulting the poisons unit and monitoring him, the nurse wrote on his discharge note, 'Patient doing well. Ready to go home. Smells good.'

A nurse went in to check on a respiratory distress patient in the Critical Care Unit who was receiving oxygen via a mask.

The nurse tried to talk to him, but all she could get out of him was gasping and unintelligible speech.

Finally, the nurse thrust a note pad and pencil at the patient and said, "I can't understand you, sir. Please write down what the problem is."

The patient weakly scrawled on the pad, "Get your foot off my oxygen tube."

A doctor informed a patient's husband that he has been informed his wife is comfortable.

The husband says, "I am surprised. I thought she was in a coma and in a critical condition."

The doctor replies, "She is, the nurses are using her as a beanbag."

A mother complained to her nurse about her daughter's strange eating habits.

She said, "All day long she lies in bed and eats yeast and car wax. What will happen to her?"

"Eventually," said the nurse, "she will rise and shine."

A dopey soldier went to see the camp nurse.

"I fell last night," he said. "And I was unconscious for eight hours."

The nurse was stunned.

She said, "How terrible. What happened?"

He replied, "I fell asleep."

A patient was wheeled into the emergency room.

The nurse asked him, "On a scale of one to ten, with one representing minimal pain and ten representing excruciating pain, what would you say your pain level is?"

He thought for a second and then said, "I don't know. I'm not very good with math."

"What do you do for a living?" a young man asked the beautiful girl he met in a bar.

"I'm a nurse," she replied.

He whispered in her ear, "I wish I could be ill and let you nurse me."

She said, "That would be miraculous. I work on the maternity ward."

"I'm so worried," the nervous patient said as the nurse plumped up his pillows.

He continued, "I recently heard about a man who was in hospital because of heart trouble and yet he died of malaria."

"Don't worry," the nurse said, smiling. "This is a first-rate hospital. If we treat someone for heart trouble, he will die of heart trouble."

A nurse says to an elderly man who is hard of hearing, "We need a stool sample and a urine sample."

The husband asks his wife, "What did she say?"

His wife replies, "They want your underwear."

The nurse was puzzled with a patient who had just been admitted.

She says, "I am very sorry Mr Murphy, but I can't diagnose your trouble. I think it must be drink."

The patient replies, "Don't worry about it. Come back later when you're sober."

A new arrival, about to enter hospital, saw two white coated nurses searching through the flower beds.

"Excuse me," he said, "have you lost something?"

"No," replied one of the nurses. "We're doing a heart transplant for an income-tax inspector and we are trying to find a suitable stone."

A man came to hospital with 70% burns.

The ward sister says to the nurse attending him, "Give him a Viagra tablet."

The nurse asks, "Do you really think that Viagra will help?"

The sister replies, "No, but it will keep the sheets off his legs."

A handsome young lad went into the hospital for some minor surgery, and the day after the procedure a friend stopped by to see how his pal was recovering.

While he was there, his friend was amazed at how many nurses entered the room in short intervals with refreshments, offers to fluff his pillows, check his temperature, make the bed and so on.

"Why are you getting all this attention?" the friend asked, "You look good to me."

The smiling patient replied, "I think the nurses formed a fan club when they heard that my circumcision required fourteen stitches."

A nurse notices a stand in the mall that says 'Brains for sale.'

She goes over to investigate and sees a sign that read, 'Paramedic brains $15 a pound, Nurses brains $30 a pound and lawyers brains $150 a pound.'

She asks the brain seller, "How come a nurse's brains are worth 30 dollars and yet a lawyer's are worth 150?"

The man replies, "Have you any idea just how many lawyers it takes to make a pound of brains?"

The hospital nurse brought a breakfast tray to a guy who was a bit of a practical joker.

The nurse also gave him a urine bottle to fill saying she'd pick it up when she came back to pick up the tray.

The patient, seeing some apple juice on the tray, decided for a bit of fun he would pour the juice into the specimen glass.

Later, when the nurse came back to pick up the specimen, she held it up to the light and said, "This looks a little cloudy. Are you feeling okay?"

The patient reached out his hand for the glass and said, "I'll run it through again, maybe I can filter it better this time." and he then drank it.

The nurse fainted.

A doctor and a nurse were called to the scene of an accident.

The doctor says, "We need to get these people to a hospital now."

The nurse asks, "What is it?"

The doctor replies, "It's a big building with a lot of medical staff."

A doctor is doing the rounds on the ward with a dyslexic nurse.

They come to a bed where the patient is laying half dead.

"Did you give this man two tablets every eight hours?" asks the doctor.

"Oh, no," replies the nurse, "I gave him eight tablets every two hours!"

At the next bed the next patient also appears half dead.

The doctor asks, "Nurse, did you give this man one tablet every twelve hours?"

"Oops, I gave him twelve tablets every one hour," replies the nurse.

Unfortunately at the next bed the patient is well and truly deceased, not an ounce of life.

"Nurse," asks the doctor, "did you prick his boil?"

"Oh My Goodness!" replies the nurse.

A nurse was showing some student nurses through the hospital.

She says to the junior nurses, "This will be the most hazardous section in the hospital for you. The men on this floor are almost well."

The hospital nurse brought a breakfast tray to a guy who was a bit of a practical joker.

The nurse also gave him a urine bottle to fill saying she'd pick it up when she came back to pick up the tray.

The patient, seeing some apple juice on the tray, decided for a bit of fun he would pour the juice into the specimen glass.

Later, when the nurse came back to pick up the specimen, she held it up to the light and said, "This looks a little cloudy. Are you feeling okay?"

The patient reached out his hand for the glass and said, "I'll run it through again, maybe I can filter it better this time." and he then drank it.

The nurse fainted.

Mick's wife was ready to give birth so he drives her to the hospital.

When he gets there the nurse in the maternity ward questions him, "How dilated is she?"

Mick replies, "Oh Jaysus, we're both over the moon."

A man went to see his doctor because he was suffering from a miserable cold.

His doctor prescribed some pills, but they didn't help. On his next visit the doctor gave him a shot, but that didn't do any good.

On his third visit the doctor told the man, "Go home and take a hot bath. As soon as you finish bathing throw open all the windows and stand in the draft."

"But doc," protested the patient, "if I do that, I'll get pneumonia."

"I know," said the doctor, "I can cure pneumonia."

A nurse tells her patient who is struggling with his breathing, "Breathe in deeply and slowly exhale, and do it three times in total."

The patient does as he is requested.

The nurse asks, "What do you feel now?"

He replies, "Your perfume is simply over-powering."

A man goes to the eye doctor. The receptionist asks him why he is there.

The man complains, "I keep seeing spots in front of my eyes."

The receptionist asks, "Have you ever seen a doctor?" and the man replies, "No, just spots."

A retired nurse was walking along the road one day when she happened to see a frog.

She reached down, picked the frog up, and started to put it into her pocket.

As he did so, the frog said, "Kiss me on the lips and I'll turn into a handsome prince."

The old nurse carried on putting the frog in her pocket.

The frog croaked, "Didn't you hear what I said?"

The nurse looked at the frog and said, "Yes I did, but at my age I'd much rather have a talking frog."

Chapter 4: Longer Nurse Jokes

Following Orders

A doctor briefed a nurse on a patient's condition.

The doctor said, "This patient is a good golfer. His injury is serious and I fear he will not be able to play golf again unless you follow my orders exactly."

The doctor then began listing orders, "You must give an injection in his left leg every 90 minutes, followed by a second injection exactly five minutes after the first. He must take two pills exactly every hours, followed by one pill every 15 minutes for eight hours. He must drink no more and no less than 10 ounces of water every 30 minutes. Every two hours, soak his arm in warm water for 15 minutes, and then place on ice for 10 minutes. He requires a back rub every hour. Feed him a low sugar low carb meal three times a day. Chart his condition and vital signs every 20 minutes. You must do these things exactly or his injury will not heal properly, and he will not able to play golf again."

The doctor left and the nurse entered the patient's room to be greeted by anxious family members and an equally anxious patient.

The patient asked what the doctor had said and the nurse replied, "The doctor said that you will live."

She then quickly added, "But you will have to learn a new sport."

The Parrot and the Nurse

A community nurse is visiting an elderly lady for the first time.

The old lady introduces the nurse to Dozy her Doberman and Precious her parrot.

After a couple of hours, the little old lady says she's going to the grocery store.

The nurse asks the little old lady if the Doberman is really dozy, and she smiles and says: "Yes. Dozy is so quiet for such a big strong dog. You can pet and talk to her if you want"

The frail old lady then adds, "But whatever you do, do NOT say anything to the parrot!"

After a couple of hours the lady excuses herself to go to the toilet.

Whilst she is gone, the parrot starts making a horrible din and starts calling the nurse all manner of rude names.

The nurse is upset, and she glares at the bird and screams, "Be quiet, you annoying bird."

The bird is stunned into silence.

A few seconds later, the parrot squawks, "Stick it to him, Dozy!"

Mischievous Grandmothers

Two mischievous grandmothers were sitting on a bench outside a nursing home.

When a grandpa walked by, one of the grandmothers yelled, "We bet we can tell exactly how old you are."

The old man said, "There is no way you can guess that you old fools."

One of the grandmas said, "Sure we can! Just drop your pants and under shorts and we will tell you your exact age."

The old guy was embarrassed but keen to prove the ladies couldn't do it, he promptly dropped his drawers.

The grandmas asked him to first turn around a couple of times.

Then they both piped up and said, "You are 82 years old."

Standing with his pants down around his ankles, the old gent asked, "How in the world did you guess?"

Laughing out loud, the two old ladies said, "Because we came to your birthday party yesterday."

Three New Babies

A maternity nurse was walking through the maternity ward, checking on the mothers and their new babies.

In the first room she met a woman who was holding a beautiful newly born child. She asked the mother what the baby's name was, to which the mother replied, "I have named her Daisy because when I went into labour, a tiny daisy drifted in through the window and landed on my tummy."

In the second room she saw another beautiful baby being held close by her proud mother. She asked the mother the name of the new arrival, to which the mother replied, "I have named her Rose because when I went into labour a small soft rose petal drifted in through the window and landed on my tummy."

In the third room she saw a mother with a baby who looked far less angelic than the other two babies she had just seen. Being polite, the nurse asked the mother what she had named her child, to which the mother replied, "I have named her Brick."

A Familiar Face

Two nurses are working at a children's hospital.

While they are checking on their patients, they notice a familiar looking man, with long straggly hair and a beard, wearing a doctor's coat walk into the ward.

Without saying anything to the nurses, he moved around the room, healing all the children with just hand gestures.

He then quickly left the ward.

As he walked by the nurses, they both noticed that the mystery man is also wearing sandals.

One nurse says to the other, "Are you thinking what I'm thinking? Was that... Jesus?"

The second nurse replies, "You could be right. I didn't recognize him at first because he wasn't wearing his usual clothes."

The first nurse states, "Maybe he was blessing in disguise."

New Nursing Technique

A new nurse at the hospital is assigned to take the vitals of the patients on the floor, with a senior nurse assigned to check her work.

The new nurse talks about how her nursing school is really pushing modern techniques and she can't wait to start using them in her work.

The new nurse takes the first patient's blood pressure, and pulse, and then she pulls up his gown and puts her finger into his rectum. After ten seconds, she pulls it out and writes something on his chart.

The senior nurse reminds her to take the patient's temperature to which she replies that she has already written it on the chart. The senior nurse decides to use her rectal thermometer and double checks and finds that the temperature written down is correct.

They go to the next patient and the process is repeated. Measure blood pressure, pulse, and then insert finger up the bottom. The senior nurse pulls out her rectal thermometer again and double checks the measurements. Once again, the temperature is right.

After repeating the process once more, the senior nurse says, "It's impressive what you have done but the only reliable way to get a core temperature is to use a rectal thermometer."

The new nurse says, "This is one of those new medical techniques. Instead of using those old slow rectal thermometers, nowadays we just use digital."

St. Peter and the Three Nurses

Three nurses died and were met at the Pearly Gates by St. Peter.

To the first, he asked, "What did you do on Earth and why should you be let into Heaven?"

"I was a nurse in an inner city hospital," she replied. "I worked in a stressful environment bringing peace and helping heal poor suffering children."

St Peter said, "That was very noble of you, you may enter Heaven."

To the next nurse, he asked the same question, "So what did you do on Earth?"

"I was a nurse at a missionary hospital in Africa," she replied. "For many years, I worked with a skeleton crew of medical staff nurses who tried to reach out to many people with a hand of healing and with a message of God's love."

St Peter said, "That was very decent of you, you may enter Heaven."

To the last nurse, he asked the same question, "So, what did you do on Earth?"

After some hesitation, she explained, "I was a case manager at an HMO."

St. Peter thought about this for a moment, and then said, "Okay, you may enter Heaven."

"Phew!" said the nurse. "For a moment, I thought you weren't going to let me in."

"Oh, you can come in," said St. Peter, "but you can only stay for five days."

The Last Will

Patrick was on his deathbed and knew the end was near.

His nurse, his wife, his daughter and two sons are with him at his home in Dublin.

He begins to speak:

"My son Michael, I want you to take the houses on Dawson Street."

"My daughter Caitlin, I want you to take the apartments at Newbridge Avenue."

"My son Seamus, I want you to take the offices on the Business Park."

As Patrick slips away, the nurse says to his wife, "Mrs. O'Reilly, my deepest condolences. Your husband must have been a hard-working and wonderful man to have accumulated all this property."

"Property, my foot," his wife replies. "The so and so had a window cleaning round."

Three Wishes

A nursing assistant, a floor nurse and a charge nurse from a small nursing home were all having their lunch break outside in the garden when they come across an old, tarnished brass lamp.

Sure enough, after rubbing the lamp, a genie comes out and grants them three wishes, one for each of them.

The nursing assistant eagerly says, "I would like to go to Antigua and have a handful of single, handsome young guys feeding me fruit and tending to my every need."

The genie waves his hand and with a puff of smoke and a flash of light, the nursing assistant is gone.

The floor nurse then says, "I wish I was in a warm, cosy lodge at a ski resort in Austria with a handful of well-groomed guys feeding me wine and cheese."

The genie also grants the floor nurse her wish, waves his hand and with another puff of smoke and a flash of light, she is gone too.

There was yet another puff of smoke and the floor nurse too was gone.

The genie turns to the charge nurse and says, "What would you like?" to which she replies with a grin, "Let me finish my lunch break and then I want those two back inside the nursing home doing their work."

Patel's Accident

There was once a Gujarati living in Florida named Raju Patel, who was involved in a car accident. At the hospital, when he awoke, he called for the nurse to tell him what had happened to him.

The nurse said, "I'm very sorry, sir, but you were involved in a serious car accident."

"Accident! Is my Mercedes all right?" he asked hysterically.

The nurse said, "I am sorry but your car was destroyed. However that is the least of your worries - you lost your left arm in the crash, and we were unable to save it."

He screams, "I lost my arm? My Rolex! My Rolex!"

The nurse says, "Please calm down. That is the least of your worries. You remain in a critical condition, but all your family are here to see you, and they are waiting outside."

He asked for his family to be called in.

As they gathered around the bed, he called for each of them by name.

"Shilpa, are you here?"

"I am here husband, and I will never leave you."

"Anil, my child, are you here?"

"I am here father, and I will never leave you."

"Dilip, my child, are you here?"

"I am here father, and I will never leave you."

"Priya, my child, are you here?"

"I am here father, and I will never leave you."

"Well," said Raju thoughtfully, "if Shilpa, Anil, Dilip and Priya are here, who the heck is in the shop?"

Three New Fathers

Three expectant fathers were in a Minneapolis hospital waiting room while their wives were in labor.

The nurse arrived and proudly announced to the first guy, "Congratulations. You're the new father of twins."

The guy said, "What a coincidence. I work for the Doublemint Chewing Gum Company."

Later the nurse returned and congratulated the second father on the birth of his triplets.

The guy said, "Well, how about that? I work for the 3M Corporation."

After this, the others turned to look at the third guy who promptly fainted.

The nurse rushed to his side to bring him round and comfort him.

As he slowly gained consciousness, the others heard him whisper, "I need some fresh air. I work for 7-Up."

A Postcard From Italy

A doctor had been having an affair with a nurse for a couple of years.

One day, she told him that she had a test and was pregnant.

Not wanting his wife to know, he gave the nurse some money and told her to go to Italy and have the baby there.

She agreed and asked, "How will I let you know when the baby is born?"

He replied, "Send me a postcard and write 'spaghetti' on the back."

One day, some six months later, the doctor's wife called him at the office and said, "Darling, you have received a strange postcard in the mail from Europe, and I don't understand what it means."

The doctor said, "I will read it when I get home later."

Later that evening, the doctor came home, read the postcard, and immediately collapsed with a heart attack.

Paramedics rushed him to the hospital.

The lead medic comforted the wife and asked what trauma had precipitated the cardiac arrest.

So the wife explained he had simply read the postcard.

The medic was puzzled so he read the postcard out loud, "Spaghetti, Spaghetti, Spaghetti - Two with sausage and meatballs, one without."

Chapter 5: Rude and Risqué Nurse Jokes

If you are easily offended, it's best to skip this chapter.

A husband and wife, both nurses, had a big argument at breakfast about their sex life.

"Let me tell you, you aren't very good in bed." the husband shouted before he stormed off to work.

By the afternoon, he decided he'd better make amends and he phoned home to apologize to his wife.

After many rings, she picked up the phone.

He asked, "What took you so long to answer?"

She replied, "I was in bed."

He asked, "What were you doing in bed at this time of day?"

She replied, "Getting a second opinion."

A friend of mine decided to have a prostate test carried out while he was visiting Thailand.

He was asked to strip off and to lay naked on his side on the couch.

After he had done so, the nurse began the examination.

After a minute, the nurse said, "At this stage of the procedure it's quite normal to get an erection."

My friend said, "I haven't got an erection."

"Well I have," replied the nurse.

I applied to be a sperm donor and the nurse asked if I could masturbate in the cup.

I told her that I'm pretty good but I don't think I am ready to compete in a tournament yet.

A nurse in a mental institution goes to check up on one of the patients and finds him sitting up in bed, pretending to be driving a car.

She asks, "Everything OK, Harry?"

Harry replies, "Sorry, but I can't talk right now. I'm busy driving into London for a meeting."

So the nurse closes the door and goes to check on Simon in the next room.

She finds Simon sitting up in his bed, w@nking furiously.

The nurse demands, "What on earth are you doing?"

Simon grunts, "I'm f*cking Harry's wife. He's gone to London."

I went to see the nurse this morning for my annual check-up.

She told me that I would have to stop masturbating.

I asked, "Why?"

She replied, "Because I'm trying to examine you."

"Of course I won't laugh," said the nurse. "I'm a professional. In over twenty years I have never laughed at a patient."

"OK then," said the patient.

He then proceeded to undo his trousers and underwear, revealing the smallest penis the nurse had ever seen in her life.

The nurse was simply unable to control herself, and she giggled.

Feeling awful that she had laughed at the man's private parts, she said, "I'm very sorry; I don't know what came over me. On my honour as a nurse, I promise it won't happen again. Now tell me, exactly what is the problem?"

The patient replied, "It's swollen."

The nurse ran out of the room.

A guy was in a hospital, in terrible pain, having just regained consciousness after an operation.

He was in the hospital's Intensive Care Unit with tubes in his nose, needles and IV drips in both arms, a breathing mask, and many wires attached monitoring a number of functions

He opened his eyes to see a gorgeous nurse hovering over him.

The nurse looked him straight between the eyes, and spoke to him in a very serious voice, slowly and clearly enunciating each word, "You may not feel anything from the waist down."

Somehow he managed to mumble a reply, "Then can I feel your tits?"

A nurse was making her rounds at the insane asylum.

Her first stop is a man with his dick in his hands and was swinging it like a baseball bat.

She asks, "What are you doing?"

He replies, "I'm Babe Ruth, the world's most famous baseball player."

She continues to the next room where she sees the patient holding his dick like a golf club.

She asks, "What are you doing?"

He replies, "I'm Tiger Woods, the world's most famous golfer."

On to the next room she peeks in and she sees a guy balancing a peanut on the tip of his dick.

She asks, "Who are you supposed to be?"

He replies, "Who me? I'm just f*cking nuts."

Chapter 6: Overheard on the Ward

I have done enough charting to navigate around the world.

You take a blue and yellow pill every day, Sir? Well, that narrows it down.

I finally got eight hours of sleep. It took me three days though.

I wish there was a cure for stupid.

Don't mess with me. I get paid to inject people.

I've seen more private parts than a hooker.

All bleeding stops ... eventually.

Being a nurse is like riding a bike. Except the bike is on fire.

Relax, I'm a nurse, I've seen a lot worse.

Remember, I'm a nurse. You're going to have to say a lot to gross me out.

Why do we have to give change of shift reports at the patients' bedsides? Won't they hear us?

I came. I cared. I charted.

I'm a nurse. I'm here to save your butt, not kiss it.

No, RN does not stand for 'Refreshments and Narcotics'"

Hand sanitizer has become one of my best friends.

Since I started nursing school, I get less sleep at night than you get during a nap.

Yes I am a nurse. No, I do not want to look at it.

You think Mondays are bad? Try working weekends, holidays and 12 hour night shifts.

I've come to the realization that I'll touch anything as long as I have gloves on.

If I collapse at work, here is the list of doctors I don't want working on me.

I love being a nurse, but I mostly love wearing scrubs. They're basically professional pajamas.

Not all patients are annoying, some are unconscious.

I tried to go a whole day without talking about bowels. I failed.

Yes, I charted that I charted what I previously charted. Wait, hold on I have to chart that I told you about my charting.

If love can't cure it, nurses can.

The only chance I got to sit down today was on the toilet.

Showering won't be enough today; I'll need to be autoclaved.

You can't cure stupid, but you can sedate it.

Do you want to talk to the doctor in charge or the nurse who knows what's really going on?

You can tell when a patient is feeling better when she starts to wear makeup.

Be nice to me. I dispense the happy pills.

Chapter 7: Novice Nurse Mistakes

Whether you are a student nurse, newly qualified or have been nursing for many years, see if you recognize yourself here.

A novice nurse wants everyone to know they are a nurse.

An experienced nurse doesn't want anyone to know they are a nurse.

A novice nurse does their head to toe assessments starting at the actual head or toes.

An experienced nurse knows that all assessment criteria will be answered during a transfer to the commode.

A new nurse gets scared when a doctor yells.

An old nurse yells back.

A new nurse is excited to sign everything.

An old nurse tries not to sign anything.

A new nurse writes notes on a pad.

An old nurse writes on a napkin, at the back of their hand, or even on their forearm.

A graduate nurse throws up when the patient does.

An experienced nurse calls housekeeping when a patient throws up.

A graduate nurse wears so many pins on their name badge you can't read it.

An experienced nurse doesn't wear a name badge for liability reasons.

A novice nurse spends hours giving a bed bath.

An experienced nurse lets the nursing assistant do a bed bath.

A graduate nurse will spend all day trying to reorient a patient.

An experienced nurse will chart the patient is disoriented and restrain them.

A graduate nurse can hear a beeping I-med at 50 yards.

An experienced nurse can't hear any alarms at any distance.

A graduate nurse loves to hear abnormal heart and breath sounds.

An experienced nurse doesn't want to know about them unless the patient is symptomatic.

A graduate nurse charts too much.

An experienced nurse doesn't chart enough.

A graduate nurse thinks people respect nurses.

An experienced nurse knows everybody blames everything on the nurse.

A graduate nurse expects meds and supplies to be delivered on time.

An experienced nurse expects them to never be delivered at all.

A graduate nurse looks for blood on a bandage hoping they will get to change it.

An experienced nurse knows a little blood never hurt anybody.

A new nurse will spend days bladder training an incontinent patient.

An experienced nurse will insert a Foley catheter.

A new nurse thinks psychiatric patients are fascinating.

An old nurse thinks psychiatric patients are simply nuts.

A novice nurse always answers the phone.

An experienced nurse checks the caller ID before answering the phone.

A graduate nurse carries reference books in their bag.

An experienced nurse carries magazines, lunch, and some "cough syrup" in her bag.

Chapter 8: Nurse Patient Exchanges

Nurse: Are you sexually active?

Patient: No, I just lay there.

Patient: I think I'm suffering from Déjà vu.

Nurse: Didn't I see you the other day?

Patient: My son has swallowed my pen, what should I do?

Nurse: Use a pencil until I get there.

Patient: I feel like a pack of cards.

Nurse: I'll deal with you later.

Patient: I think I'm a bell.

Nurse: Take these and if it doesn't help give me a ring.

Patient: I've got wind. Can you give me something?

Nurse: Yes – here's a kite.

Patient: I have a problem with these pills you gave me for BO.

Nurse: What's wrong with them?

Patient: They keep slipping out from under my arms.

Patient: I think I'm a moth.

Nurse: So why did you come here?

Patient: I saw a light at the window.

Patient: I keep getting pains in the eye when I drink coffee.

Nurse: Have you tried taking the spoon out?

Patient: Have you got something for a bad headache?

Nurse: Yes. Take this hammer and hit yourself in the head. Then you'll have a bad headache.

Patient: I see spots before my eyes.

Nurse: Did the new glasses help?

Patient: Yes, I now see the spots much clearer.

Patient: I've had a stomach ache since I ate that cheese.

Nurse: Did it smell funny when you unwrapped it?

Patient: I was supposed to unwrap it?

Patient: I keep seeing an insect spinning around.

Nurse: Don't worry; it's just a bug that's going around.

Patient: I feel run down.

Nurse: What makes you say that?

Patient: The tire marks across my legs.

Patient: I keep thinking there are two of me.

Nurse: One at a time please.

Patient: I feel like an apple.

Nurse: We must get to the core of this.

Patient: I keep losing my temper with people.

Nurse: Tell me about your problem.

Patient: I just did, you stupid fool.

Patient: My sister here keeps thinking she's invisible.

Nurse: What sister?

Patient: I feel like a racehorse.

Nurse: Take one of these every four laps.

Patient: When I donate blood I do not extract it. A nurse does it for me.

Nurse: Yes, but this is a sperm bank and it doesn't work that way.

Patient: Will this ointment clear up my spots?

Nurse: I never make rash promises.

Nurse: I have some good news and some bad news. The bad news is, you have partial short-term memory loss.

Patient: Oh no. What's the bad news?

Patient: Can I have a second opinion?

Nurse: Of course, come back tomorrow.

Patient: What can you give me for flat feet?

Nurse: How about a bicycle pump?

Patient: I keep thinking I'm invisible.

Nurse: Who said that?

Patient: I keep thinking I m a snake about to shed its skin.

Nurse: Why don't you go behind the screen and slip into something more comfortable.

Patient: Will I be able to play the piano after this operation?

Nurse: Yes, of course.

Patient: That's great because I couldn't play it before.

Nurse: Your cough sounds better today.

Patient: It should, I practised all night.

Patient: I tend to flush a lot.

Nurse: Don't worry it's just a chain reaction.

Patient: I keep thinking I'm a bee.

Nurse: Buzz off. Can't you see I'm busy?

Patient: I swallowed a bone.

Nurse: Are you choking?

Patient: No, I really did.

Patient: I'm boiling up.

Nurse: Just simmer down.

Patient: You have to help me out.

Nurse: Certainly, which way did you come in?

Patient: My hair keeps falling out. Have you got anything to keep it in?

Nurse: How about a cardboard box?

Patient: I keep painting myself gold.

Nurse: Don't worry, it's just a gilt complex.

Patient: I've broken my arm in two places.

Nurse: Well, don't go back to those places.

Patient: I think I'm a dog.

Nurse: How long have you felt like this?

Patient: Ever since I was a puppy.

Patient: I've swallowed a teaspoon.

Nurse: Sit down and don't stir.

Patient: I think I'm a yo-yo.

Nurse: Are you stringing me along?

Patient: I dream there are monsters under my bed, what can I do?

Nurse: Saw the legs off your bed.

Patient: My little boy has swallowed a roll of film.

Nurse: Let's hope nothing develops.

Patient: I feel like a hundred dollar bill.

Nurse: Go shopping. Change would do you good.

Patient: I feel like a pair of curtains.

Nurse: Well pull yourself together then.

Patient: I'm becoming invisible.

Nurse: Yes, I can see you're not all there.

Patient: I keep thinking I m a frog.

Nurse: What's wrong with that?

Patient: I think I'm going to croak.

Patient: Some days I feel like a tee-pee and other days I feel like a wig-wam.

Nurse: You're too tents.

Nurse: You seem to be in excellent health. Your pulse is as regular as clockwork.

Patient: That's because you've got your hand on my watch.

Patient: Everyone keeps ignoring me.

Nurse: Next please.

Nurse: The doctor is so funny he'll soon have you in stitches.

Patient: I hope not - I only came in for a checkup.

Patient: I get heartburn every time I eat birthday cake.

Nurse: Next time, take the candles off.

Patient: I keep dreaming of bugs, creepy-crawlies, demons, ghosts, vampires and werewolves and yetis.

Nurse: Do you always dream in alphabetical order?

Patient: I'm on a diet and it's making me irritable. Yesterday I bit someone's ear off.

Nurse: Oh dear, that's a lot of calories.

Patient: I'm a burglar.

Nurse: Have you taken anything for it?

Nurse: Good news. You have passed your hearing test.

Patient: Huh?

Patient: I keep thinking I'm a dog.

Nurse: Sit on the couch and we will talk about it.

Patient: But I'm not allowed up on the couch.

Patient: I keep hearing a ringing sound.

Nurse: Then answer the phone.

Patient: I've a split personality.

Nurse: Well, you'd better both sit down then.

Patient: You've taken out my appendix, my gall bladder, my tonsils and my varicose veins, but I still don't feel well.

Nurse: That's quite enough out of you.

Nurse: Would you like an appointment for next week?

Patient: No, I'm sick now.

Patient: I've got bad teeth, foul breath and smelly feet.

Nurse: Sounds like you've got Foot and Mouth disease.

Patient: I keep thinking I'm a caterpillar.

Nurse: Don't worry you'll soon change.

Patient: I've lost my memory.

Nurse: When did this happen?

Patient: When did what happen?

Patient: Everyone thinks I'm a liar.

Nurse: I can't believe that.

Patient: Have you got anything for my liver?

Nurse: How about some onions?

Patient: How can I cure my sleep walking?

Nurse: Sprinkle tin-tacks on your bedroom floor.

Patient: I'm having trouble with my breathing.

Nurse: I'll give you something that will soon put a stop to that.

Patient: My daughter believes in preventative medicine.

Nurse: Oh, really?

Patient: Yes, she tries to prevent me from making her take it.

Patient: Will it hurt me?

Nurse: Only when you get the bill.

Patient: I feel like a needle.

Nurse: I see your point.

Patient: I think I swallowed a pillow.

Nurse: How do you feel?

Patient: Down in the mouth.

Patient: What did the x-ray of my head show?

Nurse: Absolutely nothing.

Patient: I can't get to sleep.

Nurse: Sit on the edge of the bed and you'll soon drop off.

Patient: You've got to help me – I just can't stop my hands shaking.

Nurse: Do you drink a lot?

Patient: Not really. I spill most of it.

Patient: I feel like a dog.

Nurse: Sit!

Patient: If I give up wine, women, and song, will I live longer?

Nurse: Not really. It will just seem longer.

Patient: I think I'm a bridge.

Nurse: What's come over you?

Patient: Six cars, a truck and a bus.

Patient: I think I'm an electric eel.

Nurse: That's shocking.

Patient: I keep seeing double.

Nurse: Please sit on the couch.

Patient: Which one!

Patient: I keep thinking I'm a woodworm.

Nurse: How boring for you.

ER Nurse: So, what brings you here?

Patient: An ambulance.

Nurse: Did you know that there are more than 1,000 bones in the human body?

Receptionist: Shhh. There are three dogs outside in the waiting room.

Receptionist: There is a man in the waiting room with a glass eye named Brown.

Nurse: What does he call his other eye?

Chapter 9: Straight From Nurses' Notebooks

This is a collection of notes, as written by various nurses:

Patient has left her white blood cells at another hospital.

On the second day the knee was better and on the third day it disappeared.

The patient has been depressed since she began seeing me in 1993.

She stated that she had been constipated for most of her life until she got a divorce.

She has no rigors or shaking chills, but her husband states she was hot in bed last night.

Discharge status: Alive, but without my permission.

Patient had waffles for breakfast and anorexia for lunch.

While in ER, the patient was examined, x-rated and sent home.

Skin: somewhat pale, but present.

Patient has two teenage children, but no other abnormalities.

Mr. Murray slipped on the ice and apparently his legs went in separate directions in early December.

Patient was seen in consultation by Dr. Evans, who felt we should sit on the abdomen and I agree.

Examination of genitalia revealed he is circus-sized.

Patient was found in bed with her power mower.

The patient refused autopsy.

The patient has no previous history of suicides.

She is numb from her toes down.

Chapter 10: Nurse Pick-Up Lines

I'm an expert at mouth-to-mouth.

Have you heard what my heart is saying?

Just in time! The nurse from the previous shift took my breath away.

I want to be an organ donor? I want to give my heart to you.

You should get your own temperature. You look hot.

When we first met I couldn't get you out of my mind, now I can't get you out of my heart.

I need to practice my trauma assessments. Will you be my patient?

Do you have an inhaler? You took my breath away.

I can find every pulse in your body.

I wish I was your coronary artery, so that I could be wrapped around your heart.

Are you my appendix? I don't understand how you work, but this feeling in my stomach makes me want to take you out.

Are you a conditioned stimulus? Because you're making me drool.

Chapter 11: Bumper Stickers For Nurses

Proud to be a nurse.

Be kind to nurses. We keep doctors from killing you!

Nurses call the shots.

Nurses are I.V. Leaguers.

Hug a nurse. You'll feel better.

Cute enough to stop your heart. Smart enough to resuscitate it.

Eat. Sleep. Save lives. Repeat.

Brains of a Doctor. Heart of a Nurse.

Save Lives. Be a Nurse.

Property of a hot nurse.

Nurses may not be angels, but they are the next best thing.

Born to be a nurse.

Doctors practice. Nurses know what they are doing.

Nurses do it for twelve hours straight.

About the Author

Chester Croker, known to his friends as Chester the Jester or Croker the Joker, has written many joke books, and has twice been named Comedy Writer of the Year by the International Jokers Guild. During his schoolboy days he took voluntary service as a hospital porter and he is the significant other of a wonderful nurse, who has provided him with plenty of material for this book.

I hope you enjoyed this collection of nurse jokes. As you know, some were cheesy but I hope they brought a smile to your face, and you found them *humerus* and they tickled *your funny bone*.

If you did enjoy the book, kindly leave a review on Amazon so that other nurses can have a good laugh too.

Thanks in advance.

Final Word:-

"I attribute my success to this; I never gave nor took any excuse." - *Florence Nightingale*